Let's LEARN about the JEWISH HOLIDAYS

discover, explore and play

Let's LEARN about the JEWISH HOLIDAYS

discover, explore and play

by
ROBERT GARVEY
illustrated by
Arthur Friedman

KTAV PUBLISHING HOUSE, INC.

ISBN 87068-660-7

MV85

TABLE OF CONTENTS

Let's LEARN about the JEWISH HOLIDAYS

discover, explore and play

MITZVAH

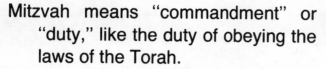

Mitzvah means "commandment" or "duty," like the duty of obeying the laws of the Torah.

Mitzvah also means doing *any* good
   deed, like helping people who need
   your help:
   giving food to someone who is hungry,
   guiding a blind person across the
   street,
   giving your seat to an old man or
   woman on a bus,
   being quiet when someone has to
   sleep,
   holding the door open for someone
   with packages.

Can you think of other mitzvot you could
   do?

MITZVAH

מִצְוָה

mitz-vah

Underline the correct answer.

A *mitzvah* is a _____.
- **good deed**
- **menorah**
- **meal**

Who can do a *mitzvah*?
- **only a professor of Hebrew**
- **only a very religious person**
- **anybody**

If you do a good deed you will _____ .
- **become rich**
- **become famous**
- **feel good inside**

The time to do a *mitzvah* is _____.
- **in the synagogue**
- **when you are told to**
- **anytime, anywhere**

Who is doing a mitzvah? Draw a line under the pictures where a mitzvah is being done.

9

THE TZEDAKAH BOX

I am the little *tzedakah* box in your home.
Put money in me to help
pay for Hebrew schools,
keep up hospitals,
plant trees in Israel.

When is a good time to put money in me?
Before your mother lights the candles for Shabbat;
on Purim, as part of *shalach manot;*
on the afternoon before Yom Kippur; anytime.
A good idea is to save some money to put in me every single week.

You'll be doing a *mitzvah*—and you'll feel good about it.

My Hebrew Dictionary

TZEDAKAH

צְדָקָה

tz-dak-ah

Underline the correct answer.

You put _____ in a *tzedakah* box.
- **sox**
- **a *siddur***
- **money**

What you put in a *tzedakah* box will be used for _____.
- **movies**
- **ice cream**
- **things like Hebrew schools and planting trees in Israel**

When you have put something into the *tzedakah* box you should _____.
- **boast about it**
- **enjoy the good feeling**
- **take something out for yourself**

A good time to put money into the *tzedakah* box is _____.
- **when you are older**
- **now and every week**
- **when you are rich**

Tzedakah money is used to help people. To which group of people would you give tzedakah? Underline the tzedakah pictures.

THE MEZUZAH

I am the *mezuzah* on your doorpost. I am a small, thin box, made of wood or metal.

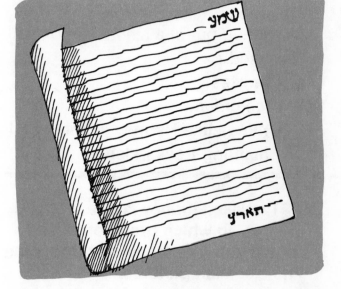

Whenever you look at me, remember. Remember that God wants you to keep His Commandments so that you can live a long and happy life.

Inside me is a tiny piece of parchment with the words, in Hebrew: *Shema Yisrael, Adonai Elohenu, Adonai Echad . . . (Hear, O Israel, the Lord our God, the Lord is One! And you shall love the Lord your God with all your heart and with all your soul and with all your might. And these words which I command you this day shall be upon your heart. . . . And you shall write them upon the doorposts of your house, and upon your gates . . .)*

My Hebrew Dictionary

מְזוּזָה

m'zoo-zah

MEZUZAH

Underline the correct answer.

The words of the *mezuzah* are

_____ .

- **written by hand**
- **typewritten**
- **finger-painted**

A *mezuzah* should remind you to

_____

- **go fishing**
- **keep the Commandments**
- **eat a cookie**

A *mezuzah* can be seen on the

_____ of a Jewish home.

- **piano**
- **ceiling**
- **doorpost**

Inside the *mezuzah* are the words

_____.

- **"I Have a Little Draydl"**
- **"One Potato, Two Potato"**
- ***"Shema Yisrael ..."***

Draw a line from the word to the picture.

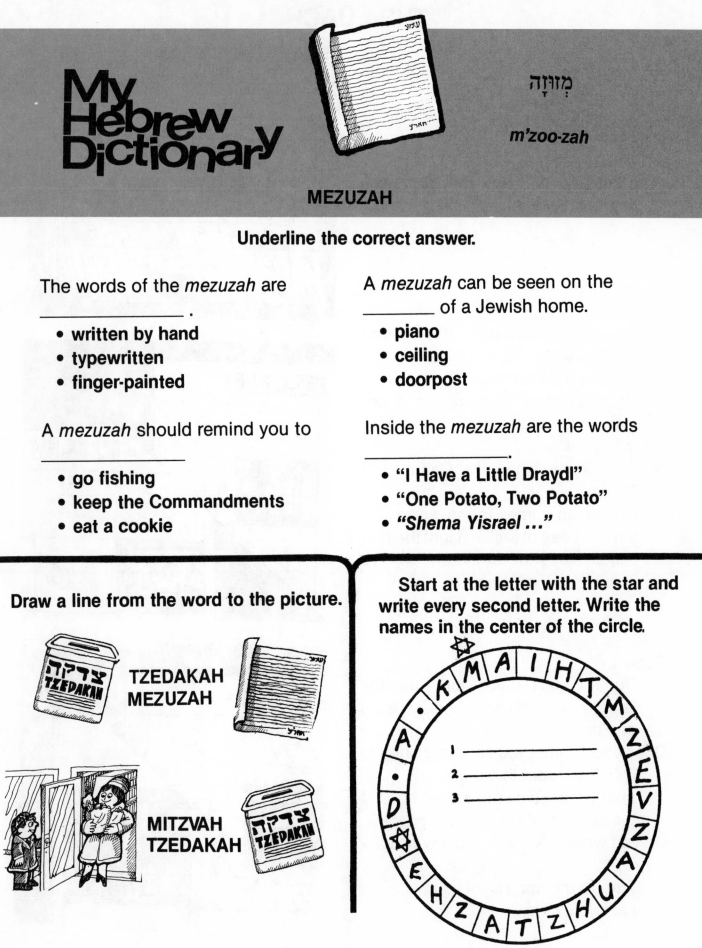

TZEDAKAH
MEZUZAH

MITZVAH
TZEDAKAH

Start at the letter with the star and write every second letter. Write the names in the center of the circle.

1 _____
2 _____
3 _____

13

THE LUACH

I am the Jewish calendar. I am called
luach in Hebrew.

Do you want to know when it is Pesach
(Passover)?
Look at me and read:
Pesach comes in the spring. It be-
gins on the 15th day of the Hebrew
month, Nisan.
Want to know when it's Chanukah?
Read:
Chanukah comes in the winter, on
the 25th day of Kislev. Light the first
candle in your menorah on the
evening of the 24th.

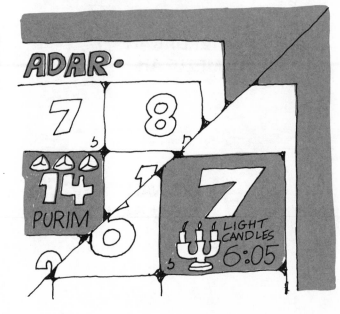

Purim?
Purim comes almost three months
later, on the 14th day of Adar. It lasts
one day.
Does your mother want to know when to
light the Sabbath candles?
Look here. This Friday evening light
the candles at five minutes past six.
Do you want to know when any holiday
is?
Turn to me and I'll tell you.
I am your *luach.*

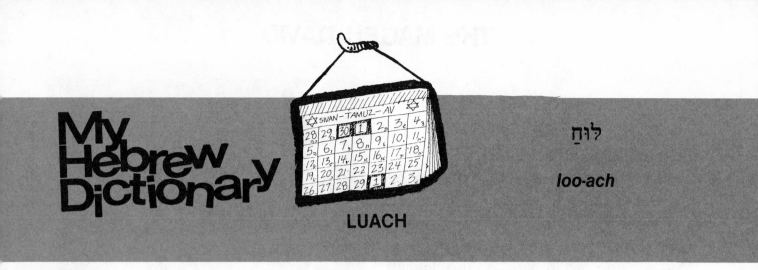

LUACH

לוּחַ

loo-ach

Draw a line from the word to the picture.

**TZEDAKAH
LUACH**

**TZEDAKAH
MITZVAH**

**LUACH
MITZVAH**

Underline the correct answer.

If you want to know when a Jewish holiday is, look it up in the _____.
- **telephone book**
- **encyclopedia**
- *luach*

If you went to a Jewish book store and asked for a *luach* they would give you a _____.
- **Jewish calendar**
- **Bible**
- *Megillah*

The *luach* tells you not only the English days and months but also the _____ days and months.
- **Greek**
- **Hebrew**
- **Japanese**

THE MAGEN DAVID

I am a *Magen David.*
Take two triangles and place one on top
    of the other to make a six-pointed
    star—that's me.
I'm not a star in the sky, though.
You will see me in blue, on the Jewish
    flag.

You may see me outside the
    synagogue, and inside—
    on a menorah,
    on the curtain of the Ark,
    on a kiddush cup,

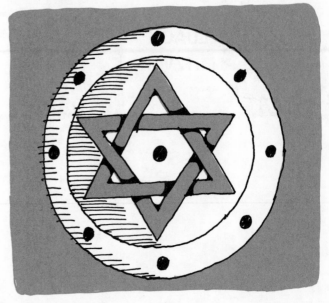

People call me the Shield of David.
They think of me as a symbol of the
    Jewish religion.

Draw a line from the word to the picture.

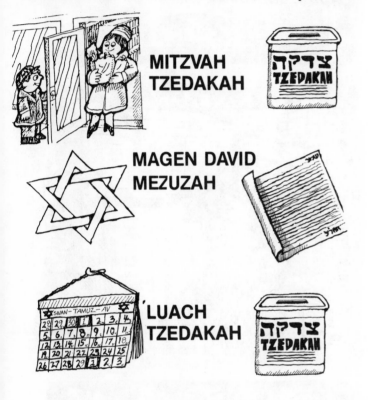

MITZVAH
TZEDAKAH

MAGEN DAVID
MEZUZAH

LUACH
TZEDAKAH

Underline the correct answer.

The *Magen David* is _____.
- a five-pointed star
- a movie star
- the Shield of David

You are sure to see a *Magen David* at
_____ .
- the Yankee Stadium
- any synagogue or temple

The *Magen David* is a symbol of the
_____ .
- Jewish religion
- Pennsylvania Dutch
- Soviet Union

How many Magen Davids can you find in this picture?

17

THE ISRAELI FLAG

I am the Israeli flag.
See my two blue stripes and *Magen David*?

In Israel I fly everywhere—from flag-
poles in the parks, schools, hospitals, and other buildings.

In this country I fly with the flags of the
United Nations and at Israel Independence Day parades.

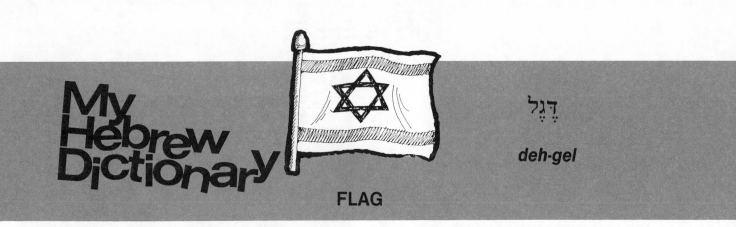

My Hebrew Dictionary

דֶּגֶל

deh-gel

FLAG

Draw a line from the word to the picture.

ALEFBET
FLAG

MAGEN DAVID
MEZUZAH

MEZUZAH
TZEDAKAH

Underline the correct answer.

The Israeli flag has _____.
- **two blue stripes and a *Magen David***
- **three red strips and a gragger**
- **a star, a sun and five moons**

In Israel the Israeli flag flies _____.
- **nowhere • everywhere**
- **only at the *Knesset***

In the United States you can see the Israeli flag in _____.
- **the Israel Independence Day parades and at the United Nations**
- **every bus station • every gym**

Below you will find a box of letters. Find and circle the words in the word list. The words can be found by reading forwards, up and down and on the diagonal.

**ALEFBET,
FLAG,
LUACH,
TZEDAKAH,
MAGEN DAVID.**

B	F	A	U	T	I	F	L
A	L	E	F	B	E	T	U
I	A	M	A	G	E	N	A
N	G	D	A	V	I	D	C
T	Z	E	D	A	K	A	H

19

THE ALEFBET

I am the *alefbet*, the Hebrew alphabet.
My letters are:

    *alef, bet, vet, gimel, dalet, hay, vav,
zayin, chet, tet, yod, kaf, chaf,
lamed, mem, nun, samech, ayin,
pay, fay, tzadi, kof, resh, shin, sin
tav*

    ....twenty—six letters in all.

vav	hay	dalet	gimel	vet	bet	alef
ו	ה	ד	ג	ב	ב	א

lamed	chaf	kaf	yod	tet	chet	zayin
ל	כ	כ	י	ט	ח	ז

tzadi	fay	pay	ayin	samech	nun	mem
צ	פ	פ	ע	ס	נ	מ

tav	sin	shin	resh	kof
ת	שׂ	שׁ	ר	ק

You can make any Hebrew words you
    want with my letters.
    Put an *alef* and a *mem* together and
you have mother *(aim).*

Put an *alef* and a *vav* together and
you have father *(av).*

20

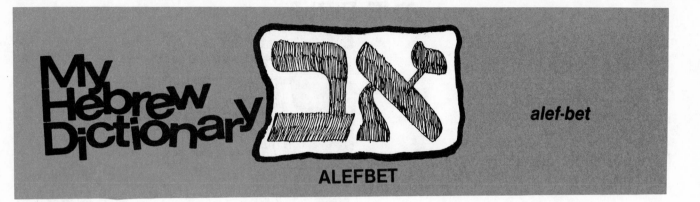

My Hebrew Dictionary

alef-bet

ALEFBET

Underline the correct answer.

There are _____ letters in the *alefbet*.
- **26**
- **57**
- **101**

The first two letters are _____.
- *alef* and *lamed*
- *fay* and *bet*
- *alef* and *bet*

You read Hebrew from _____.
- **left to right**
- **right to left**
- **bottom to top**

Put an *alef* and a *mem* together and you have the word _____.
- *aim*
- **May**
- **Mimi**

How many hidden alefs can you find in this picture?

21

THE BIBLE

I am the Bible, the Holy Scriptures, the
Tanach.

Actually, I am not one book but 39
books.
I have three parts:
The Five Books of Moses, or The
Law (*Torah* in Hebrew);
The Prophets (*Naviim* in Hebrew),
21 books;
The Writings (*Chetuvim* in Hebrew),
13 books.
Put the Hebrew initials of my three
parts together and you get the word
TaNaCH. That is my name in He-
brew.

My books are all about God and the
Jewish people.
Read me! Study me! Learn how to live
from me!

My Hebrew Dictionary

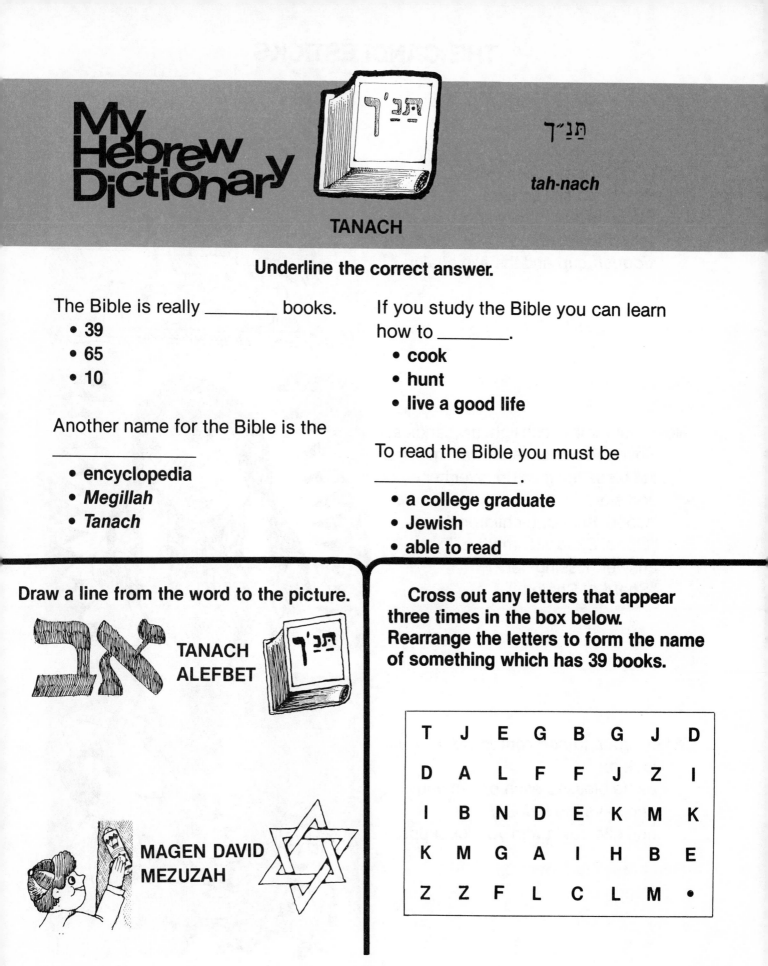

תַּנַ"ךְ

tah-nach

TANACH

Underline the correct answer.

The Bible is really _____ books.
- **39**
- **65**
- **10**

Another name for the Bible is the

_____
- *encyclopedia*
- *Megillah*
- *Tanach*

If you study the Bible you can learn how to _____.
- **cook**
- **hunt**
- **live a good life**

To read the Bible you must be

_____.
- **a college graduate**
- **Jewish**
- **able to read**

Draw a line from the word to the picture.

TANACH
ALEFBET

MAGEN DAVID
MEZUZAH

Cross out any letters that appear three times in the box below.
Rearrange the letters to form the name of something which has 39 books.

T	J	E	G	B	G	J	D
D	A	L	F	F	J	Z	I
I	B	N	D	E	K	M	K
K	M	G	A	I	H	B	E
Z	Z	F	L	C	L	M	•

THE CANDLESTICKS

I am the Sabbath candlesticks.
  Polish me till I sparkle.
  Place me on the white tablecloth
  with the bottle of wine and the
  kiddush cup and the two *chalot*.

Now your mother can light my candles.
  Covering her eyes she will murmur
  the blessing, then uncover her eyes
  and say,
  "Good Shabbat, children."
  "Good *Shabbat*, mother," you will
  answer, kissing her,
  "*Shabbat Shalom*."

When your father comes home I will
  look on
  as he blesses each one of you
  and says the *Kiddush*
  and sits down with you for supper.

My Hebrew Dictionary

פָּמוֹטִים
pah-moh-tim

CANDLESTICKS

Underline the correct answer.

Sabbath candlesticks are _____.
- candles and sticks
- candleholders for Sabbath eve
- silver to lock in a safe

After Mother lights the candles she says: _____.
- "Happy Birthday!"
- "Happy New Year!"
- "Good *Shabbat*, children."

You answer Mother: _____.
- "Let's play *draydl*."
- "Where are the *hamantashen*?"
- "Good *Shabbat*, Mother, *Shabbat Shalom*."

Father blesses you then recites _____
- the *Kiddush*
- "Little Jack Horner"
- "Mary Had a Little Lamb"

DOWN

ACROSS

Complete the crossword puzzle by filling in the English names.

4

8

21

3

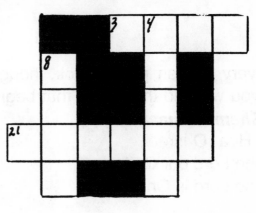

THE SIDDUR

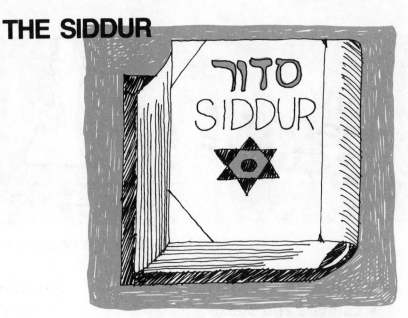

I am a *siddur,* a prayer book.

Read from me every day of the week.
Follow my words when the rabbi and
 cantor lead the prayers on *Shabbat.*
For special *Shabbats* and Jewish holidays there is a prayer book with
 special prayers.
It is called a *machzor.*

In every Jewish prayer book, though,
 you will find the prayer that begins
 Shema Yisrael,
 "Hear, O Israel,
 the Lord our God,
 the Lord is One!"

My Hebrew Dictionary

סִדּוּר

sih-dur

SIDDUR

Draw a line from the word to the picture.

**SIDDUR
CANDLESTICKS**

**TANACH
ALEFBET**

**ALEF
BET**

Underline the correct answer.

The *siddur* is a prayer book for _____
- **everyday and the Sabbath**
- **Rosh Hashanah and Yom Kippur**
- **Chinese New Year**

"Hear, O Israel, the Lord our God, the Lord is One!" is in every Jewish _____ book.
- **cook**
- **geography**
- **prayer**

The special prayer book for Jewish holidays is called a _____.
- *Megillah*
- *Haggadah*
- *machzor*

Below you will find a box of letters. Find and circle the words in the word list. The words can be found by reading forwards, up and down and on the diagonal.

MEZUZAH

SIDDUR

ALEF

TZEDAKAH

FLAG

M	E	Z	U	Z	A	H	L
S	I	D	D	U	R	A	A
U	S	E	L	E	S	L	S
G	F	L	A	G	E	E	P
A	R	T	H	U	E	F	E
T	Z	E	D	A	K	A	H

THE TALIT

I am a *talit,* a prayer shawl.
I am made of wool or silk, with black or
    blue stripes. There are fringes *(tzi-
    tzit)* at each of my four corners, to
    remind you to keep the Command-
    ments.

I am worn in the synagogue.
When you are thirteen years old, you
    too may wear a *talit*.

On Simchat Torah all the children under
    thirteen go up to the *bimah,* and a
    large *talit* is spread above them as
    they repeat the Torah blessing and
    receive a blessing from the rabbi.

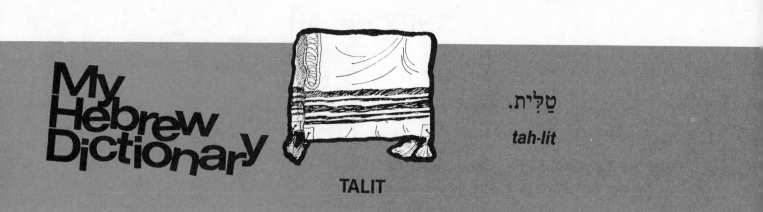

My Hebrew Dictionary

TALIT

טַלִּית.

tah-lit

Underline the correct answer.

A *talit* is _____.
- **a Purim noisemaker**
- **good with butter and jam**
- **a prayer shawl**

When you wear a *talit*, people will think you are _____.
- **saying your prayers**
- **on television**
- **doing your homework**

On _____ children at synagogue gather under a large *talit*.
- **Passover**
- **Simchat Torah**
- **Chanukah**

You usually wear a *talit* in the synagogue after you are _____.
- **married**
- **65 years old**
- ***Bar Mitzvah***

Draw a line from the word to the picture.

FLAG
LUACH

TALIT
SIDDUR

How many children are under the talit?

THE CHALAH

I am the two braided loaves (*chalot*) of bread on the Sabbath table. Near me are the *kiddush* cup and a bottle of wine.

While we wait here,
   your mother lights the candles,
   your father comes home and welcomes the *Shabbat* and blesses each one of you
   and says the *Kiddush.*

He sits down at the table with you. He says the *motzi* blessing over me and passes a slice of *chalah* around for everybody to eat.

My Hebrew Dictionary

CHALAH

חַלָּה

chah-lah

Underline the correct answer.

A *chalah* is a _____.
- bagel without a hole
- braided loaf of bread
- *hamantash* without jam

Chalah is usually eaten on _____.
- **Pesach**
- **Tu Bishevat**
- **Shabbat**

Friday evening the table is set with *chalah* and _____.
- *matzot*
- a *kiddush* cup and candles
- a *mezuzah*

The _____ blessing is said over the *chalah*.
- **Torah**
- *shofar*
- *motzi*

Draw a line from the word to the picture.

TALIT
CHALAH

MAGEN DAVID
MEZUZAH

On Shabbat we greet our family, friends and neighbors by saying, "*Shabbat Shalom.*"

"*Shabbat Shalom*" means "Good Sabbath".

Stand up and shake hands with your friend and say, "*Shabbat Shalom.*"

A KIDDUSH CUP

I am the *kiddush* cup.
Go ahead, father: fill me up and say the
    Kiddush—the blessing over my
    wine.

Now why does everyone look so
    happy?
    Is it because your loving family is
    here and everything has a *Shabbat*
    look—
    the table with the white cloth
    the lighted candles
    the two *chalot*
    the freshly-cut flowers
    —all in honor of the Sabbath?

Now that you have said the *Kiddush*,
    father, let everyone have a sip of
    my wine.
Good *Shabbat*, family! *Shabbat
Shalom*!

My Hebrew Dictionary

גְבִיעָה

g'vee-ah

KIDDUSH CUP

Draw a line from the word to the picture.

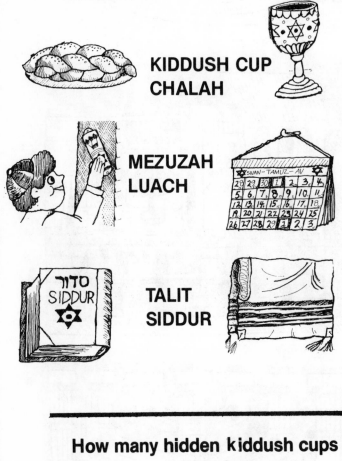

KIDDUSH CUP
CHALAH

MEZUZAH
LUACH

TALIT
SIDDUR

Underline the correct answer.

When the Sabbath table is set with the lighted candles, *chalot* and flowers, everyone looks _____.
- angry
- sad
- happy

After filling the *kiddush* cup with wine, Father _____.
- dips a slice of *chalah* into it
- carefully pours it on the tablecloth
- says a blessing over it

After the *Kiddush*, the family _____.
- does somersaults
- has a sip of the wine
- reads from the *Megillah*

How many hidden kiddush cups can you find in this picture?

33

MENORAH FOR SHABBAT

I am a menorah.

I have seven branches for seven candles.

Long, long ago the children of Israel took me with them as they wandered in the desert after leaving Egypt.

Many years later I stood in the Temple at Jerusalem until the Roman army destroyed the Temple and carried me off to Rome.

After that, wherever Jews lived, they built synagogues and I was in those synagogues.

Today you can see me in many places in Israel.

If you visit Jerusalem you can see me standing in front of the *Knesset* (parliament) building—a giant menorah, fifteen feet tall.

You can also see me in synagogues and temples everywhere in the world.

My candles are lighted every Friday evening to welcome *Shabbat.* They are lighted for other Jewish holidays too.

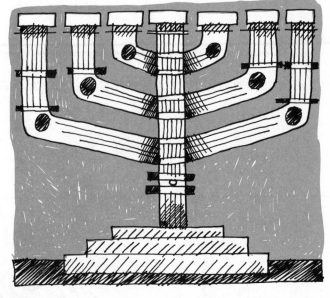

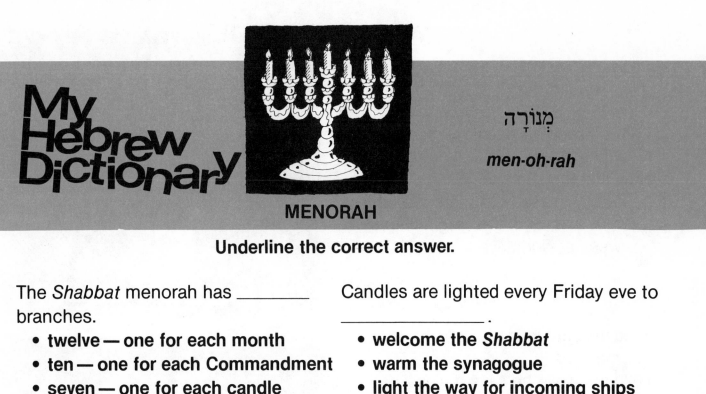

My Hebrew Dictionary

MENORAH

מְנוֹרָה

men-oh-rah

Underline the correct answer.

The *Shabbat* menorah has _____ branches.
- twelve — one for each month
- ten — one for each Commandment
- seven — one for each candle

Candles are lighted every Friday eve to _____ .
- welcome the *Shabbat*
- warm the synagogue
- light the way for incoming ships

A giant menorah stands _____.
- on the White House lawn
- outside the *Knesset*
- in the hand of the Statue of Liberty

The children of Israel carried a menorah with them after they left _____.
- their huts at night
- school
- the land of Egypt

Draw a line from the word to the picture.

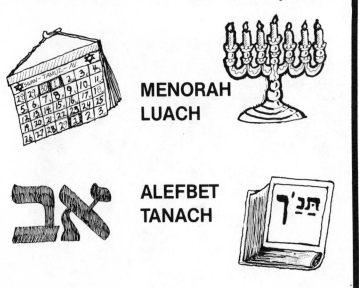

MENORAH
LUACH

ALEFBET
TANACH

Add and subtract. You will make a word describing something we eat on Shabbat.

HAVDALAH CANDLE

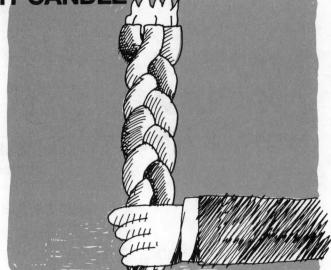

I am a *havdalah* candle with blue-and-white braids.

Now that the sun has gone down, your family is ready to mark the end of *Shabbat* and the beginning of a week of workdays.

Hold me straight while your father lights me.

Hold me while he says a blessing over the cup of wine.

Hold me while he shakes the box of spices and passes it around, letting everyone enjoy its spicy smell.

Hold me while he puts his fingers near my flame.

Now your father spills a little of the wine into a saucer and you dip my flame into it, snuffing it out.

"*Shavua Tov*!" everybody sings. "A good week—a happy week!" and everybody sips from the wine cup and gives everybody a loving hug.

36

My Hebrew Dictionary

HAVDALAH

הַבְדָּלָה

hav-dah-lah

Underline the correct answer.

The time to light the *havdalah* candle is when _____.
- the sun has gone down
- there is a blackout
- nobody is around

The *havdalah* marks the end of the _____
- Torah reading
- summer vacation
- *Shabbat*

You hold the havdalah candle in _____.
- a candlestick
- your hand
- a bowl of water

After the *havdalah* ceremony it is _____.
- the new moon
- the beginning of a new week
- time to light the *Shabbat* candles

Draw a line from the word to the picture.

HAVDALAH
CHALAH

תַּנַ"ךְ

TALIT
TANACH

Here are six spice boxes. They all look alike, but one is a little different. See if you can find it.

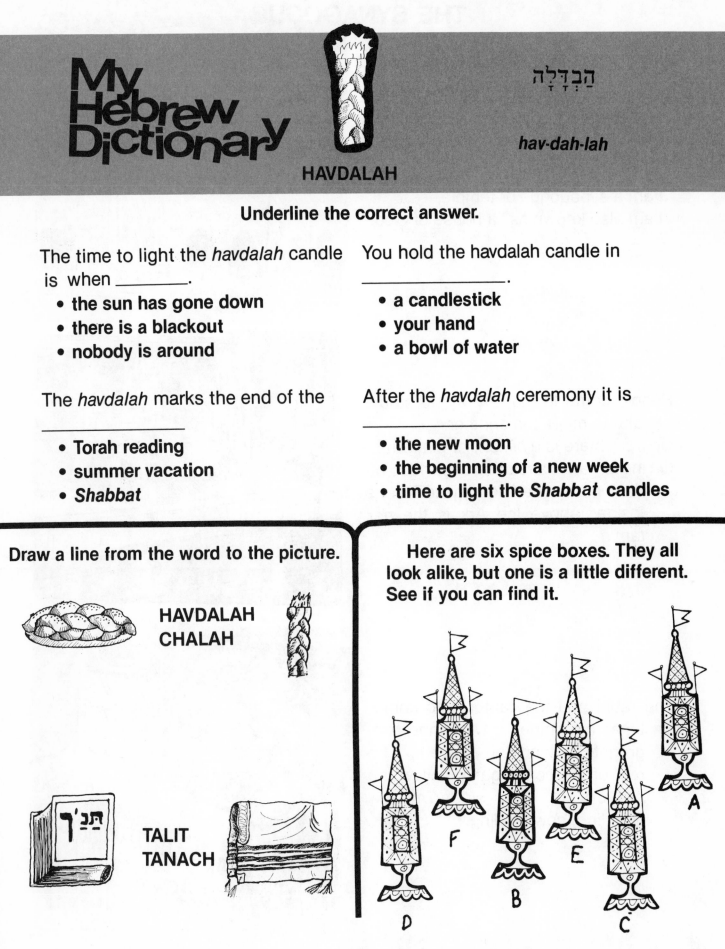

37

THE SYNAGOGUE

I am a synagogue or temple.
I am also known as "a house of God."

People come to me to pray, to study,
and to meet one another.
Up front there is a *bimah,* or platform.
On the *bimah* is a reading desk. Also on
the bimah is the Ark, with the Torahs
inside. Above the Ark is the *ner
tamid.*

The rabbi and the cantor, and sometimes a member or two of the congregation, lead the prayers. The
rest of the congregation follow the
prayers in their *siddurim,* now
chanting, now reading.

My Hebrew Dictionary

בֵּית־הַכְּנֶסֶת

bet hak-nes-et

SYNAGOGUE

Underline the correct answer.

A synagogue, or temple, is also known as _____.
- **a house of God**
- **the old opera house**
- **a movie palace**

The Ark is kept on the _____ of the synagogue.
- **balcony**
- **roof**
- ***bimah***

People come to the synagogue to _____.
- **pray**
- **play**
- **fly airplanes**

The prayers chanted in the synagogue are found in the _____.
- **morning newspaper**
- ***siddur***
- **farmer's almanac**

Draw a line from the word to the picture.

CHALAH
FLAG

SYNAGOGUE
MENORAH

This is where everybody goes on the Sabbath. Draw lines from number to number, and you will see what it is.

13• 14• 15•
12•   16•
11•   17• •18
9•   •19 •20
10

•21   •22

6   5
4   3
7   2   !
•8

THE RABBI

I am a rabbi.
Some people call me "a man of God."
Actually, the Hebrew word *rabbi* means
"my teacher."

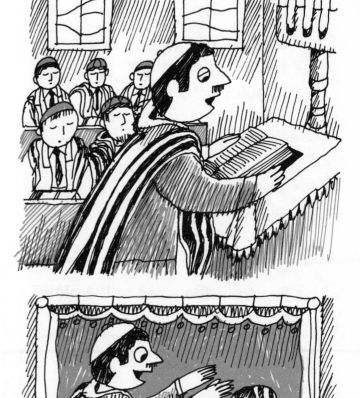

I try to teach people how to live a happy
life by following the Commandments of the Jewish religion.
I lead the prayers in the synagogue.
I give the sermon and tell children
stories from the Bible and the Tal-
mud. Sometimes I teach a class.

When you are thirteen years old, I will
bless you as a *Bat Mitzvah* or *Bar
Mitzvah*. Later I may perform your
marriage. And I may even be
present at the naming of your child.
I am your friend—your rabbi.

My Hebrew Dictionary

רַבִּי

rah-bee

RABBI

Draw a line from the word to the picture.

RABBI
TALIT

CHALAH
HAVDALAH

MAGEN DAVID
FLAG

Underline the correct answer.

If you have a question about the Jewish religion, ask _____.
- **your rabbi**   • **your lawyer**
- **your auto mechanic**

The word rabbi means _____.
- **mister**   • **my teacher**
- **king**

At your *Bat Mitzvah* or *Bar Mitzvah* ceremony your rabbi will _____.
- **stand you on your head**
- **bless you**
- **play basketball with you**

Below you will find a box of letters. Find and circle the words in the word list. The words can be found by reading forwards, up and down and on the diagonal.

CHALAH
RABBI
TALIT
BET
FLAG

R	C	H	A	L	A	H	B	F
T	A	L	I	T	O	L	A	L
A	R	B	M	A	B	E	T	A
P	A	B	B	L	O	V	E	G
S	T	R	A	I	M	E	R	S

41

THE CANTOR

I am a cantor.
Some people call me *chazan*, the Hebrew word for "singer."
I am in charge of the music of your synagogue.

I chant the Hebrew prayers and help the rabbi lead the service.
I also lead the choir.
Sometimes I train a children's choir or a choir made up of people of the congregation.

In the religious school, I teach you to chant the Hebrew prayers and to sing Jewish songs.
I am your cantor.

My Hebrew Dictionary

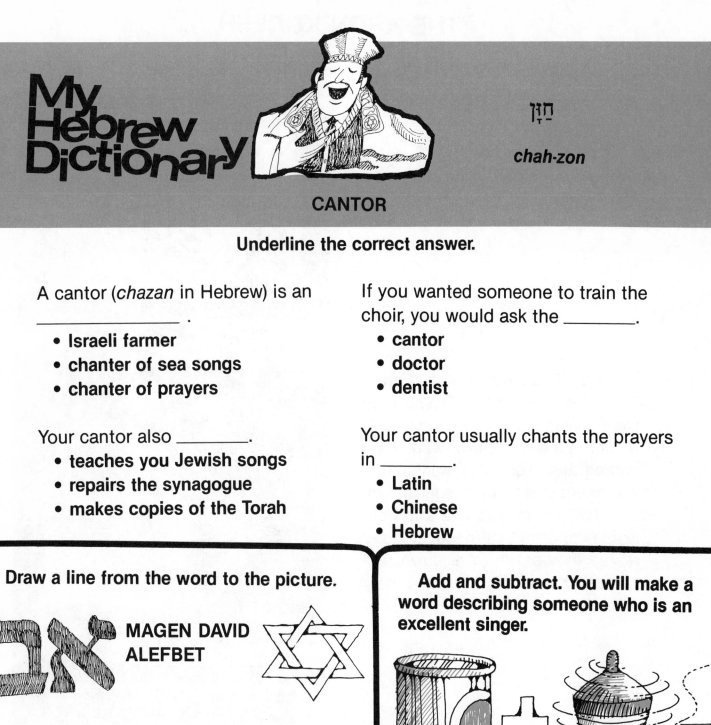

חַזָּן

chah-zon

CANTOR

Underline the correct answer.

A cantor (*chazan* in Hebrew) is an
_____ .
- Israeli farmer
- chanter of sea songs
- chanter of prayers

Your cantor also _____.
- teaches you Jewish songs
- repairs the synagogue
- makes copies of the Torah

If you wanted someone to train the
choir, you would ask the _____.
- cantor
- doctor
- dentist

Your cantor usually chants the prayers
in _____.
- Latin
- Chinese
- Hebrew

Draw a line from the word to the picture.

אָב

MAGEN DAVID
ALEFBET

CANTOR
LUACH

**Add and subtract. You will make a
word describing someone who is an
excellent singer.**

P + R =

43

THE ARON KODESH

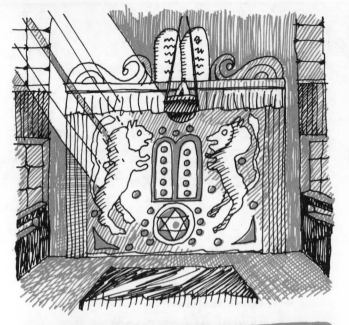

I am the *Aron Kodesh*—the Ark in the synagogue.

Once upon a time, after the children of Israel left the land of Egypt, they were given the Ten Commandments. Wherever they went they carried the Ten Commandments with them in an Ark, a special box they had made beautiful with gold inside and out. Whenever they rested they set the Ark down and put a tent around it, to make a holy place for worship.

Now an *Aron Kodesh* stands in every synagogue and the Torah (with the Ten Commandments) is kept in it.

My Hebrew Dictionary

אֲרוֹן־קֹדֶשׁ.

aron koh-desh

HOLY ARK

Draw a line from the word to the picture.

HOLY ARK
CANTOR

SYNAGOGUE
SiDDUR

Underline the correct answer.

After leaving Egypt, the children of Israel carried with them _____.
- an Ark
- a pyramid
- a golden calf

Today the *Aron Kodesh* is kept in the _____
- bedroom
- synagogue
- park

See if you can find your way to the Holy Ark?

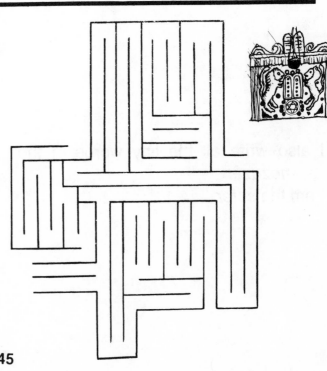

THE SOFER

I am the one who writes down the words of the Torah. I am called a *sofer,* a scribe, a writer of holy books. I use a quill when I write. I write in Hebrew, with vegetable ink, on the parchment of the Torah.

I write with great care, saying each word aloud before I write it, so that I will not make a mistake.
I write out the first five books of the Bible on the Torah scroll.

I also write all the tiny words in the *mezuzah.*
I am the *sofer.*

My Hebrew Dictionary

SOFER

סוֹפֵר

soh-fer

Underline the correct answer.

The *sofer* writes on parchment with
_____.

- crayon
- chalk
- a quill and vegetable ink

This is what the *sofer* writes on the
Torah scroll: _____.
- the *Haggadah*
- the first five books of the Bible
- poems and songs

He also writes _____.
- the Hebrew words of the *mezuzah*
- recipes for cook books
- rock songs

A *sofer* is a _____.
- musician
- writer of holy books
- scientist

Draw a line from the word to the picture.

SOFER
TORAH

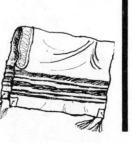

KIDDUSH CUP
TALIT

Here are four Torot. Which one is different?

A

B

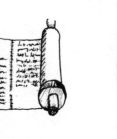

C

D

47

THE NER TAMID

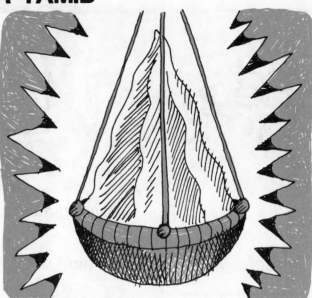

I am a little lamp in the synagogue that is always kept burning.

I hang above the Ark.
I remind you that you are in a house of God.

I remind you that the light of God's goodness never goes out.
I am also called the eternal light.
I am the *ner tamid.*

My Hebrew Dictionary

נֵר תָּמִיד

ner tah-mid

LAMP

Draw a line from the word to the picture.

NER TAMID
SOFER

HOLY ARK
TANACH

תנ״ך

Underline the correct answer.

The *ner tamid* is also called _____.
- **the eternal light** • **the lamp of wisdom**
- **the Sabbath lamp**

When you see the *ner tamid* you know you are in a _____.
- **public library**   • **radio station**
- **house of God**

The *ner tamid* reminds you that
_____.
- **without light you can't read**
- **the light of God's goodness never goes out**

DOWN   **ACROSS**

4   1

6   33

Complete the crossword puzzle by filling in the English names.

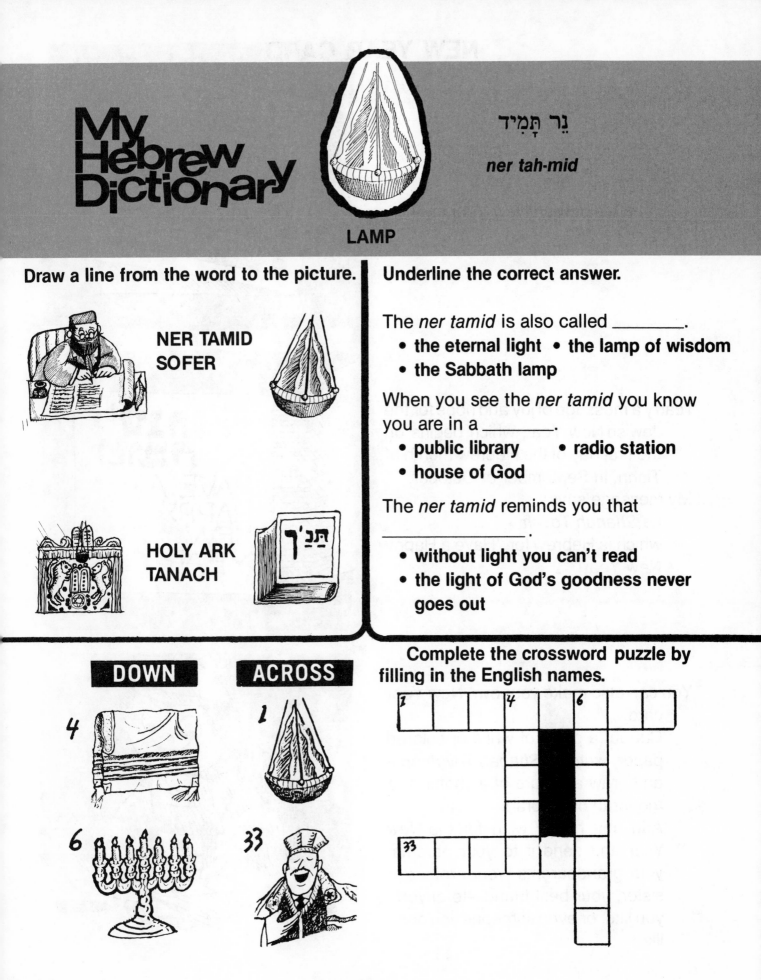

49

NEW YEAR CARD

I am a Jewish New Year card.

I carry a message of joy and hope for the Jewish New Year, which begins on the first day of the Hebrew month of Tishri, in September or October.

My message says:

Le Shanah Tovah

which is Hebrew for "Have a Happy New Year!"

You can also make your own New Year card.

Cut out a piece of white or colored paper, write *Le Shanah Tovah* on it and draw a picture of a shofar or a menorah or a Torah.

Add any happy wish for the New Year and send it to your parents, your grandparents, your brother or sister, your best friend—to anyone you like, or even someone you don't like!

50

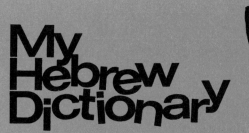
Underline the correct answer.

The special words on a Jewish New Year card are _____.
- *"Bon Voyage. Have a good trip!"*
- *"Le Shanah Tovah. Have a Happy New Year!"*
- *"Mazel Tov on your Bat Mitzvah!"*

The Jewish New Year comes _____.
- on the first day of January
- on the first day of spring
- in September or October

If you make your own New Year card, you want to draw a picture of a _____.
- *shofar*
- witch on a broom
- *havdalah* candle

A Jewish New Year card carries a message of _____.
- sorrow
- blame
- joy and hope for the new year

Draw a line from the word to the picture.

NEW YEAR CARD
NER TAMID

TORAH
LUACH

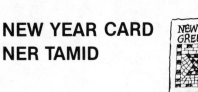

See if you can deliver this New Year card to the house.

THE SHOFAR

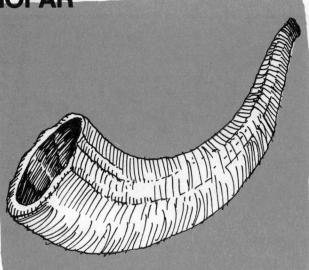

I am the *shofar,* a ram's horn.
I am sounded in the synagogue on the Holy Days of Rosh Hashanah and Yom Kippur.

"Te-ke-ah . . ." chants the cantor or rabbi, and I sound high and shrill, as if calling out to you: *Wake up! Think! Have you disobeyed the Commandments?*
Have you been mean to anyone?
Have you told lies to anybody?
Have you taken anything that belongs to someone else?
Have you refused to help somebody who needed your help?

Remember! Go to those people and tell them you are sorry. Ask them to forgive you. Promise to be a better person in the new year.

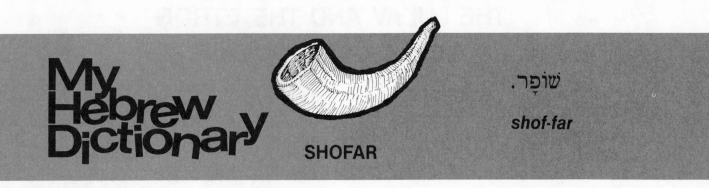

My Hebrew Dictionary

SHOFAR

שׁוֹפָר.

shof-far

Draw a line from the word to the picture.

SHOFAR
SOFER

RABBI
SIDDUR

ALEFBET
MAGEN DAVID

Underline the correct answer.

A *shofar* is a _____.
- hired driver of an auto
- ram's horn
- French horn

The *shofar* is sounded on _____.
- Purim
- Chanukah
- Rosh Hashanah and Yom Kippur

The sound of the *shofar* reminds you to _____.
- practice your violin
- run around the block
- tell anybody you have hurt that you are sorry

Add and subtract. You will make a word describing something we blow on Rosh Hashanah.

53

THE LULAV AND THE ETROG

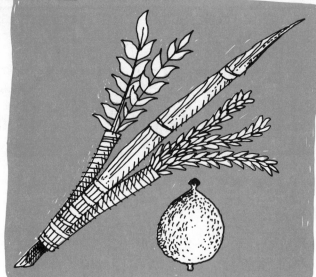

I am a *lulav,* a palm branch,
    tied with twigs of myrtle and willow
    leaves.
I am an *etrog,* a citrus fruit.
    I am yellow like a lemon, only big-
    ger.
    I have the smell of a lemon, only
    sweeter.

Lulav, etrog, myrtle and willow—we are
    four different growing things that
    you use in celebrating the festival of
    Sukot.

Hold me, the *lulav* (with myrtle and
    willow leaves),
    in your right hand; and hold me, the
    etrog,
    in your left hand. Now wave us
    together, pointing us in all direc-
    tions.
We remind you to give thanks for all the
    good things that grow.
We remind you that God's goodness is
    everywhere.

My Hebrew Dictionary

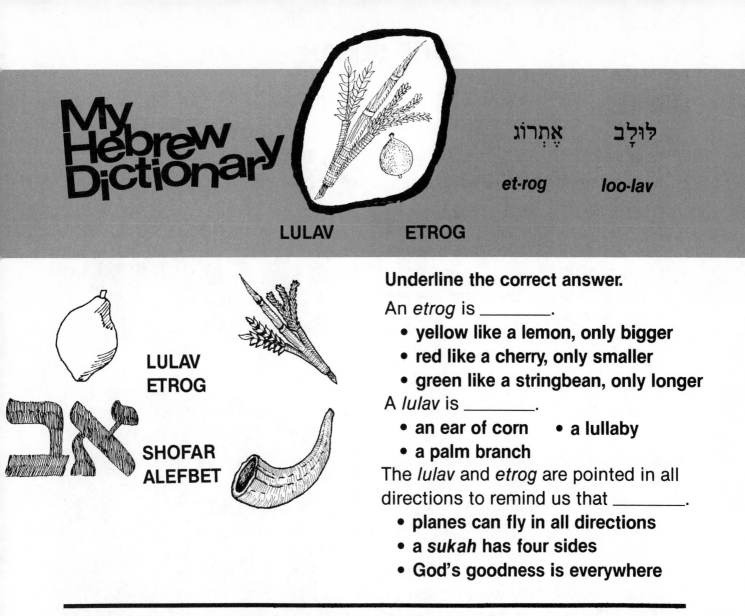

אֶתְרוֹג   לוּלָב

et-rog   loo-lav

LULAV   ETROG

LULAV
ETROG

SHOFAR
ALEFBET

Underline the correct answer.

An *etrog* is _____.
- yellow like a lemon, only bigger
- red like a cherry, only smaller
- green like a stringbean, only longer

A *lulav* is _____.
- an ear of corn   • a lullaby
- a palm branch

The *lulav* and *etrog* are pointed in all directions to remind us that _____.
- planes can fly in all directions
- a *sukah* has four sides
- God's goodness is everywhere

Below you will find a box of letters. Find and circle the words in the word list. The words can be found by reading forwards, up and down and on the diagonal.

ALEF
ETROG
LULAV
LUACH
TORAH
TALIT
ARK

L	U	L	A	V	D	O	G	H
E	M	U	L	T	R	H	A	T
T	P	A	E	A	O	A	Y	U
R	S	C	F	L	R	R	M	W
O	E	H	R	I	L	K	A	X
G	A	M	P	T	L	E	G	H

THE SUKAH

I am a *sukah,* a special hut.

    I stand in the yard of your synagogue for the week-long festival of Sukot.

    My roof is covered with branches so that you can see the stars through them at night.

    Fruits and vegetables and flowers hang from my roof.

Did you know that the children of Israel, your ancestors, lived in huts? That was after they left the land of Egypt and lived in the desert for forty years.

Did you know that when they lived in the land of Israel, they would come in out of the fields at harvest-time to rest in such huts?

Today your family can put up a *sukah* in your own yard and eat in it during Sukot.

I remind you of the huts of your ancestors. I remind you to give thanks to God for all things that grow.

You might call me a hut of thanksgiving.

My Hebrew Dictionary

סֻכָּה

soo-kah

SUKAH

Underline the correct answer.

If you build a *sukah* of your own, you should _____.

- **keep your bicycle in it**
- **eat in it on Sukot**
- **use it as a nursery to grow plants**

The *sukah*, with all the green, growing things, reminds us that _____.

- **growing things smell good**
- **we should give thanks to God for all things that grow**

After the children of Israel left Egypt they lived in _____.

- **trailers**
- ***sukahs***
- **trees**

A *sukah* is a _____.

- **watermelon**
- **Turkish pipe**
- **hut**

Start at the letter with the star and write every second letter. Write the names in the center of the circle.

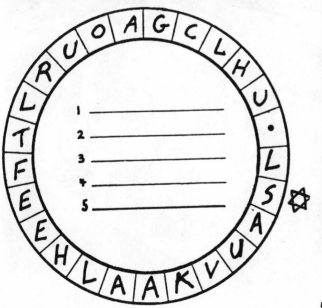

1 _____
2 _____
3 _____
4 _____
5 _____

Draw a line from the word to the picture.

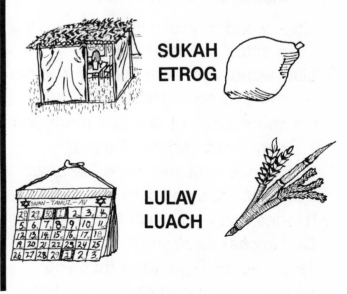

SUKAH
ETROG

LULAV
LUACH

57

THE TORAH

I am the Torah scroll.
You keep me in the Ark of the synagogue.
  You dress me in a mantle of velvet or satin with threads of gold and with a silver crown and breastplate.

I am made up of many pieces of parchment, sewn together.
  My words are in Hebrew, written by hand.
Written on me are The Five Books of Moses.
  These books tell how God created the world; how God promised Abraham that if the Jews obeyed His laws, He would always be their God. They tell how the Jews were led out of slavery by Moses. They tell how God gave Moses the Commandments on Mount Sinai.

Little wonder you call me holy, the greatest treasure of the Jews.
Little wonder you love me and read me every *Shabbat* and festival!
On the holiday of *Simchat Torah* you parade around the Temple.
You dance with me, wave *Simchat Torah* flags and sing songs.
It takes one whole year to read me.
On *Simchat Torah* you read my very last chapter. Right after that, you start me all over again and read my very first chapter.

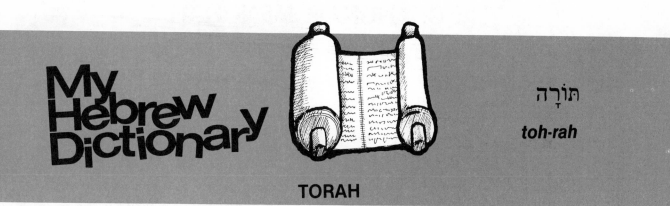

My Hebrew Dictionary

תּוֹרָה

toh-rah

TORAH

Underline the correct answer.

The Torah is read in the synagogue every _____.
- *Shabbat* and festival
- blue moon
- year on Simchat Torah

The Torah Scroll is written in _____.
- Egyptian on papyrus
- Hebrew on parchment
- Yiddish on paper

The greatest treasure of the Jewish people is _____.
- A *Magen David* with rubies and diamonds
- a golden menorah
- the Torah

The Torah is kept in _____.
- a bank in Switzerland
- a cave under Hebrew University
- the Ark of every synagogue

  **TORAH HOLY ARK**

 **SYNAGOGUE HAVDALAH**

Start at the letter with the star and write every second letter. Write the names in the center of the circle.

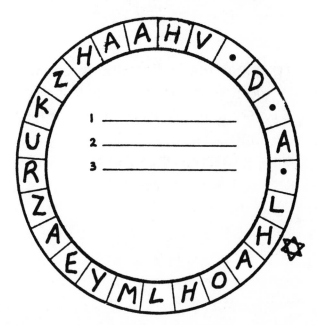

1 _____
2 _____
3 _____

THE CHANUKAH MENORAH

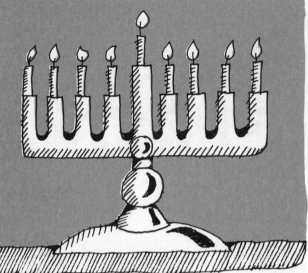

I am a Chanukah menorah. I have nine branches—for eight candles and one helper *(shamash)* candle.

Your family gathers around me to light my candles—one candle on the first night of Chanukah, two candles on the second night, and so on until the eighth night, when all my candles are lighted.

After the lighting ceremony, everybody sings the *Maoz Tsur* ("Rock of Ages").

You place me on the window sill with my lighted candles so everybody can see it is Chanukah, the Feast of Lights.

Happy Chanukah, everybody!

My Hebrew Dictionary

CHANUKAH MENORAH

חֲנֻכִּיָּה

cha-noo-kee-yah

Underline the correct answer.

A Chanukah menorah holds _____.

- **eight candles and a helper candle**
- **seven candles—one for each day of the week**
- **dozens of candles**

The lighted menorah is then placed _____.

- **on the window sill**
- **in the refrigerator**
- **in the clothes closet**

After the candles are lighted you sing _____.

- **"Pop Goes the Weasel"**
- **"Hatikvah"**
- **"Maoz Tsur"**

After the first night you light _____.

- **one candle more**
- **one candle less**
- **all the candles**

DOWN   ACROSS

✔ Complete the crossword puzzle by filling in the English names.

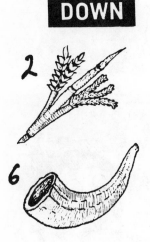

2

6

9

43

THE DRAYDL

I am a *draydl*, a Chanukah top. I have four sides. On each side is a Hebrew letter—*nun, gimel, hay,* and *shin.* The letters stand for the words, *Nes Gadol Hayah Sham* ("A great miracle happened there").

The miracle is that a flask of oil for the Temple menorah burned for eight days instead of one day. The miracle is that a small band of Maccabees fought against the Syrian army and won! They won the right to worship the true God and to keep the Sabbath.

Have the Chanukah candles been lighted? Did you sing the *Maoz Tsur?* Have you eaten your supper? Now is a good time to sit down and spin me. Play for nuts or candy coins or for anything you like.

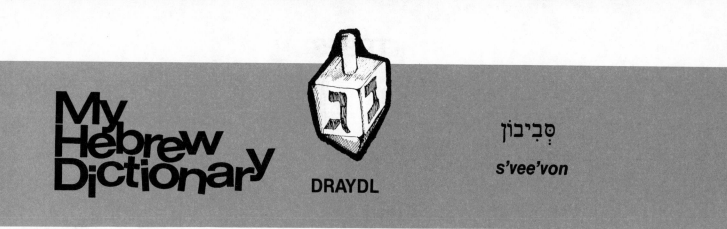

My Hebrew Dictionary

DRAYDL

סְבִיבוֹן

s'vee'von

Draw a line from the word to the picture.

**LULAV
LUACH**

**DRAYDL
CHANUKAH MENORAH**

**ALEFBET
SIDDUR**

Underline the correct answer.

A draydl has four sides. On each side is a Hebrew letter: _____.
- *nun, gimel, hay,* and *shin*
- *alef, bet, gimel,* and *dalet*
- *hay, vav, zayin,* and *chet*

The letters stand for *Nes Gadol Hayah Sham,* which means_____.
- **"A great miracle happened there"**
- **"Wait till the top stops"**
- **"Spinning tops are singing tops"**

Two miracles of Chanukah are _____.
- a *draydl* spun for eight days
- a tiny flask of oil burned for eight days
- a small band of Maccabees fought the Syrian army and won

How many draydls can you count in this pile?

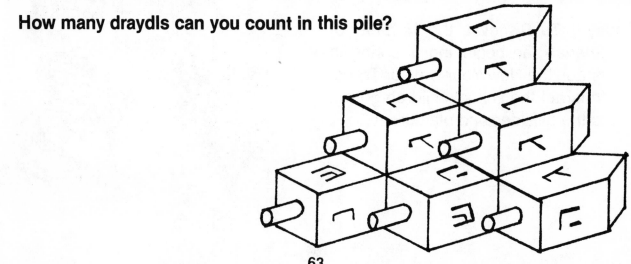

TREES

I am a tiny tree.
Dig a hole and plant me.

Here in the United States it is January or February—quite cold, and the ground is hard. So plant me indoors, in a flower box, in honor of the trees of Israel. Eat fruits that grow in Israel, like dates, figs, oranges, grapes, and fruit of the carob tree. Give money to the Jewish National Fund for the planting of trees in Israel.

Today is *Tu Bishevat,* the 15th day of *Shevat,* the beginning of spring in Israel, the New Year Day for Trees. In Israel the school children go out to the hillsides and plant trees.

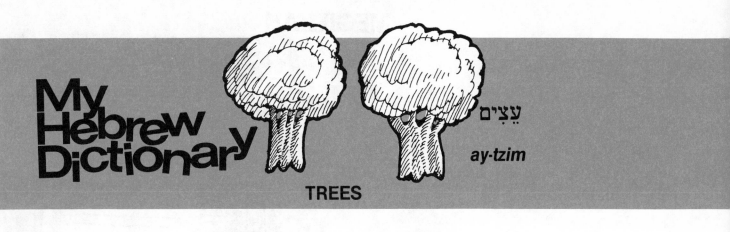
Underline the correct answer.

On *Tu Bishevat* school children in Israel go out to the hillsides to _____.
- **chop down trees**
- **count**
- **plant**

Since it is winter in America on *Tu Bishevat*, we do our planting _____.
- **indoors**
- **in the snow**
- **on an ice pond**

On *Tu Bishevat* we enjoy _____.
- **fruits**
- **chicken soup**
- **gefilte fish**

We give money to the Jewish National Fund for _____.
- **trips to Jerusalem**
- **digging new caves**
- **planting trees**

Draw a line from the word to the picture.

TREES
DRAYDL

NER TAMID
TALIT

• See if you can find your way to the tree planting place.

65

MEGILLAH

I am the *Megillah*—the scroll of Esther. On me is written the story of Purim as told in the Bible.

Watch the cantor unroll me. Listen to him read how Esther was chosen queen and how she saved her people from Haman, the wicked prime minister of Persia. When the name "Esther" is read, you can say, "Ahhhh." When "Haman" is read you can make a noise and cry "Boo!"

Make your own *Megillah,* if you like. On this scroll, print the story of Esther in your own words. Draw pictures too. A picture of Haman leading Mordecai on the king's horse through the streets of Shushan. Don't forget a picture of the Jews of Persia dancing for joy.

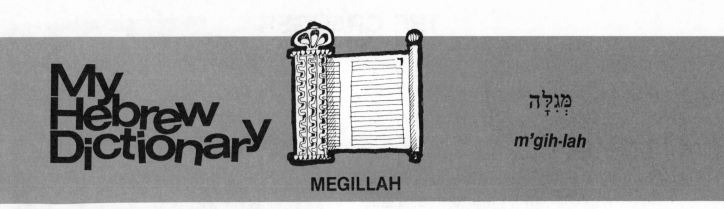

My Hebrew Dictionary

מְגִלָּה

m'gih-lah

MEGILLAH

Draw a line from the word to the picture.

SOFER TORAH

MEGILLAH DRAYDL

Underline the correct answer.

A Purim *Megillah* is a _____.
- blackboard   • scroll of Esther
- Hebrew typewriter

When the name "Haman" is read, you
_____ .
- dance for joy   • eat ice cream
- drown out his name with noise

When you make your own *Megillah*,
you might draw a picture of _____.
- Noah's Ark
- the Israelites crossing the Red Sea
- Haman leading Mordecai on the
  king's horse

✔ **Complete the crossword puzzle by
filling in the English names.**

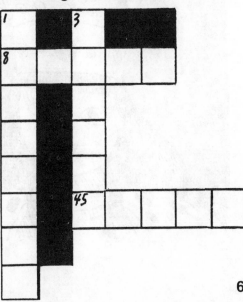

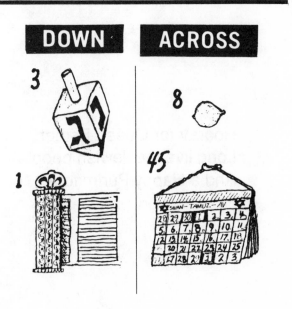

DOWN   **ACROSS**

67

THE GRAGGER

I am a Purim noisemaker—a *gragger*.
Do I speak softly or sing sweetly?
Not me! Whirl me, shake me, rattle
me—and I make a rasping, grating
NOISE.

Right in the synagogue: When you are
there on Purim night and the *Megillah* is being read, just listen for the
name of a certain wicked man . . .
Did you hear "Haman"? Quick—
whirl me, shake me, rattle me! Oh,
what a noise I make! You and I
drowned out the name of that horri-
ble Haman who wanted to kill all the
Jews of Persia.

Hooray for Queen Esther!
Long live the Jewish people!
And a Happy Purim to all!

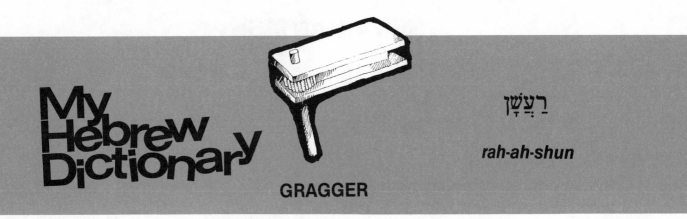

My Hebrew Dictionary

רַעֲשָׁן

rah-ah-shun

GRAGGER

Underline the correct answer.

A *gragger* is a _____ maker.
- **noise**
- **pie**
- **song**

The *gragger* is whirled on Purim in your _____.
- **street**
- **home**
- **synagogue**

You whirl the *gragger* during the reading of the _____.
- *Haggadah*
- *Megillah*
- *siddur*

The sound of the *gragger* drowns out the name of _____.
- **Mordecai**
- **Esther**
- **Haman**

Draw a line from the word to the picture.

SYNAGOGUE
TORAH

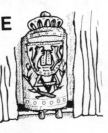

GRAGGER
MEGILLAH

Start at the letter with the star and write every second letter. Write the names in the center of the circle.

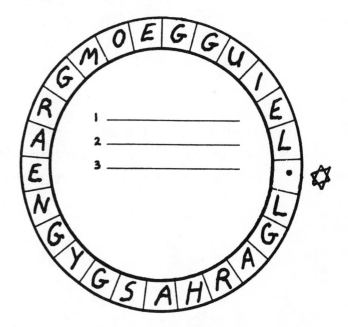

1 _____
2 _____
3 _____

69

THE HAMANTASH

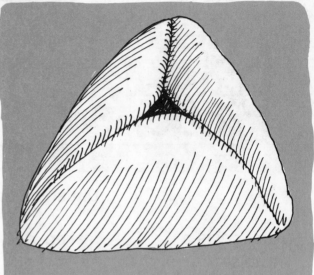

Hi, I'm a *hamantash*,
  the little three-cornered cake filled with jam or poppy-seeds-and-honey that you eat on Purim.

Were you thinking of taking somebody a bit of *shalach manot*?
  Hamantashen are exactly right—whether you bake us or buy us at the bakery.
  Take us to your friends or relatives and wish them "A Happy Purim!"

Who knows? They may give *you* something delicious in return—like pastry, cookies, or *hamantashen*!

My Hebrew Dictionary

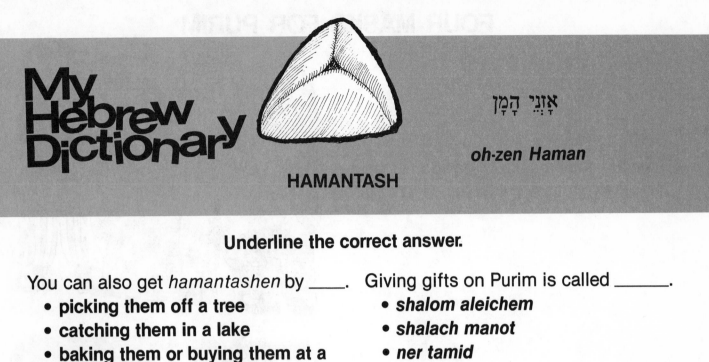

HAMANTASH

אָזְנֵי הָמָן

oh-zen Haman

Underline the correct answer.

You can also get *hamantashen* by _____.
- picking them off a tree
- catching them in a lake
- baking them or buying them at a bakery

A *hamantash* is a _____.
- pumpkin
- six-pointed star
- three-cornered cake

Giving gifts on Purim is called _____.
- *shalom aleichem*
- *shalach manot*
- *ner tamid*

_____ are perfect for *shalach manot*.
- hamantashen
- goldfish
- potato chips

Draw a line from the word to the picture.

**HAMANTASH
GRAGGER**

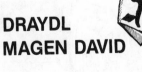

**DRAYDL
MAGEN DAVID**

How many hidden *hamantashen* can you find in this picture?

FOUR MASKS FOR PURIM

We are four masks. Wear us for your Purim masquerade—and have fun.

Put *me* on your face and you are Mordecai, a judge in Shushan. Remember! You will not bow down to Haman. You are a Jew and Jews bow down only to God.

Wear *me* and you are beautiful Esther, Mordecai's cousin. You've been chosen queen and now Mordecai has told you that your people are in danger.

Wear *me* and you are Haman, prime minister of Persia. Everyone bows down to you—except Mordecai the Jew. So you plot to get rid of him and all the Jews. You draw lots (*purim*) to decide on the day.

Wear *me* and you are Ahasuerus, king of Persia. Your new queen, Esther, has told you about Haman's wicked plot to destroy her and her people. You must help her!

My Hebrew Dictionary

MASKS

מַסֵכוֹת

mah-say-chot

Draw a line from the word to the picture.

MASKS

HAMANTASH

SIDDUR
HAVDALAH

SHOFAR
GRAGGER

Underline the correct answer.

At a Purim masquerade you wear a
_____.

- **pair of skis**
- **basket of fish on your head**
- **mask**

You dress up like _____.
- **a gorilla**
- **a tree**
- **somebody in the Purim story**

If you want to look beautiful, you wear
a mask of _____.
- **King Ahasuerus**   - **Haman**
- **Queen Esther**

Below you will find a box of letters. Find and circle the words in the word list. The words can be found by reading forwards, up and down and on the diagonal.

MASK,
SHOFAR,
HAMANTASH,
ESTHER,
HAMAN.

M	C	O	A	V	I	D	C	S
H	A	M	A	N	T	A	S	H
A	E	S	T	H	E	R	M	O
M	A	N	K	O	I	T	A	F
A	L	I	E	S	R	U	S	A
N	E	V	E	R	O	R	K	R

THE HAGGADAH

I am the *Haggadah,* the book that you read from at the *seder*.

In words and pictures I tell you the story of the children of Israel, your ancestors, who were once slaves in Egypt and who were led out of slavery to freedom.

I also tell you how to hold a *seder* in your home—
what special foods to prepare,
how to set the table,
what blessings to say,
and what songs to sing.

My Hebrew Dictionary

HAGGADAH

הַגָּדָה

ha-gah-dah

Draw a line from the word to the picture.

HAGGADAH
HAMANTASH

DRAYDL
TALIT

Underline the correct answer.

The *Haggadah* tells you how _____.
- the world began
- an *afikomen* was found
- your ancestors were led out of slavery

The *Haggadah* is _____.
- a Passover hat
- an old witch
- the book you read from at the *seder*

DOWN

23

3

ACROSS

25

1

Complete the crossword puzzle by filling in the English names.

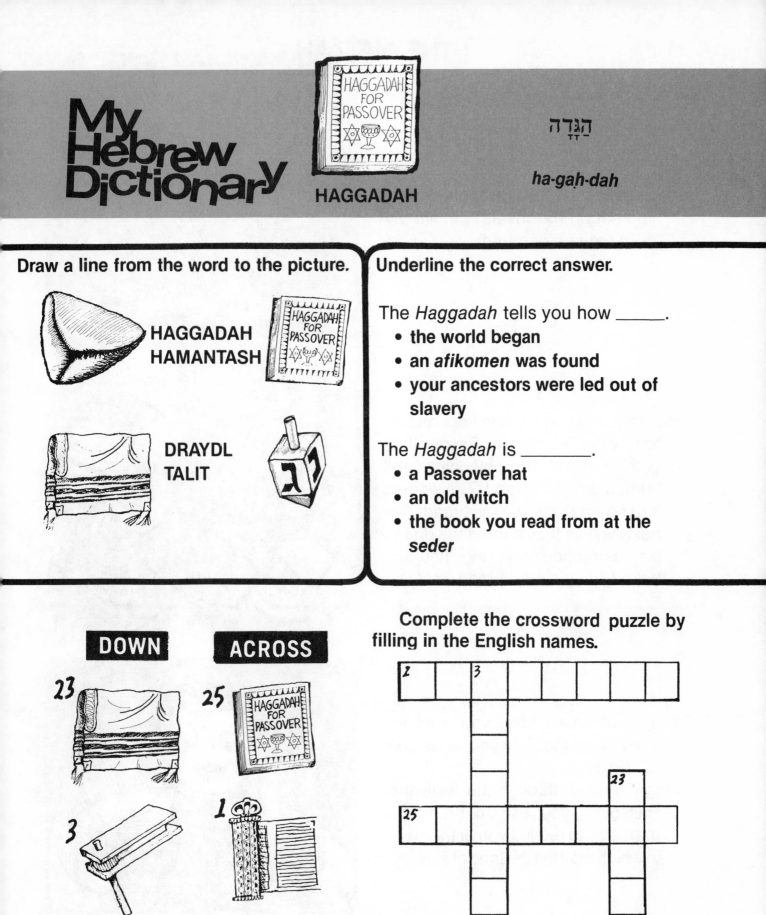

THE MATZAH

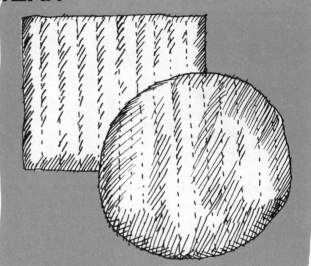

I am the *matzah*, the unleavened bread you eat on Passover. I am flat and crisp, square or round.

One night, long ago, when your ancestors were slaves in Egypt, they gathered up all their belongings and hurried out of that land. The women had no time to bake their bread. The next day, as they carried the dough on their shoulders, the hot sun baked it into a hard bread, *matzah*.

Tonight, at your *seder*, you read the story about the night your ancestors left Egypt.
Tonight, and all through the festival of Passover, you eat no bread but *matzah*—to remind you of the haste in which they left the land of slavery.

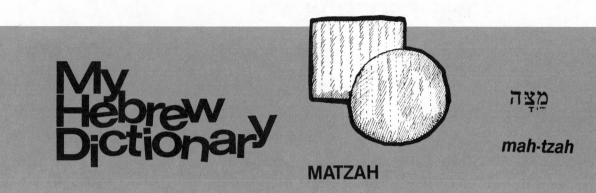
Underline the correct answer.

Matzah is _____.
- **a bagel**
- **a pizza**
- **unleavened bread**

You always eat matzah on _____.
- **July 4th**
- **April Fool's Day**
- **Pesach**

The first *matzot* were made when your ancestors _____.
- **hurried out of Egypt**
- **crossed the Red Sea**
- **were given the Ten Commandments**

Eating *matzah* reminds you _____.
- **about the haste in which your ancestors left Egypt**
- **the time Queen Esther saved her people**
- **to wear your rubbers when it rains**

Draw a line from the word to the picture.

MATZAH
HAGGADAH

CHANUKAH MENORAH
CANDLE STICKS

Add and subtract. You will make a word describing something we eat on Passover.

77

THE SEDER PLATE

I am the large and handsome plate you set before the leader of the *seder*. On me are five special things:

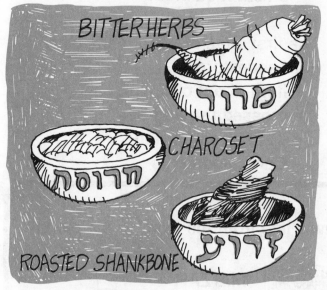

Maror or bitter herbs (root of horseradish)—to remind you of the bitter lives of your ancestors and of all people who are slaves today;

Charoset (chopped apples, nuts and raisins, mixed with cinnamon and wine)—to remind you of the cement your ancestors made bricks with, when they were slaves;

A roasted shankbone (*z'roah*)—to remind you of the offerings your ancestors brought to the Temple in Jerusalem;

BITTER HERBS — מרור
CHAROSET — חרוסת
ROASTED SHANKBONE — זרוע

Karpas (parsley or any green vegetable)—to remind you of the things that come to life each spring and of our hope for freedom everywhere in the world.

Roasted egg (*baytzah*)—a symbol of life.

Now you are ready to begin the *seder*.

KARPAS — כרפס
ROASTED EGG — ביצה

My Hebrew Dictionary

SEDER PLATE

קְעָרָה
k'ah-rah

Underline the correct answer.

In front of the leader of the *seder* is a large _____.
- **plate**
- **frying pan**
- **bowl of soup**

The _____ reminds us of the cement our ancestors made bricks with.
- **roasted shankbone**
- *matzah*
- *charoset*

The bitter herbs (*maror*) remind us of _____
- **the bitter lives of all slaves**
- **birthday cake**
- **not to chew tobacco**

The _____ reminds us of the things that come to life each spring.
- **tablecloth**
- **parsley (*karpas*)**
- **sky**

Draw a line from the word to the picture.

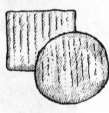

SEDER PLATE
MATZAH

GRAGGER
TORAH

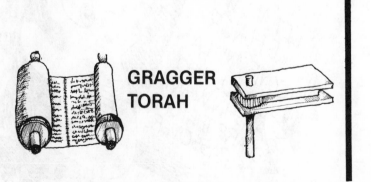

Start at the letter with the star and write every second letter. Write the names in the center of the circle.

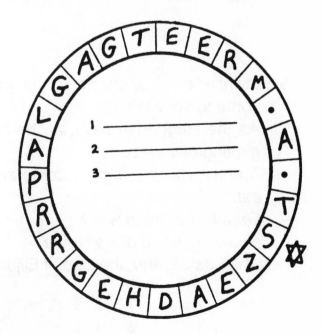

1 _____
2 _____
3 _____

79

THE CUP OF ELIJAH

I am the big cup of wine you have set out on your seder table for Elijah the Prophet.

When you open the door,
will Elijah walk in and sip from my cup?
You always hope he will, for when Elijah appears it will be the time when the whole world will live in peace and freedom.

Meanwhile, any hungry person is welcome to your table.
As the Haggadah says, at the beginning of your *seder*:
*"Let all who are hungry come and eat.
Let all who are in want
share the hope of Passover."*
I am the *Kos Eliyahu,* the Cup of Elijah.

My Hebrew Dictionary

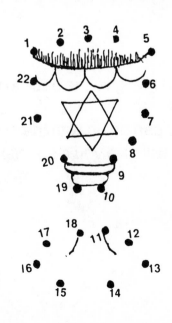

כּוֹס אֵלִיָּהוּ

kos Eh-lee-ya-hoo

CUP OF ELIJAH

Draw a line from the word to the picture.

CUP OF ELIJAH
SEDER PLATE

MATZAH
HAGGADAH

ALEF
SUKAH

Underline the correct answer.

When Elijah comes the whole world will _____.
- **have peace**
- **go to war**
- **eat** *matzah*

The Cup of Elijah is filled with

_____
- **water**
- **wine**
- **pickles**

Kos Eliyahu means _____.
- **Elijah's Cup** • **Elijah's football**

This is what Elijah drinks from. Draw lines from number to number, and you will see what it is.

81

AFIKOMEN

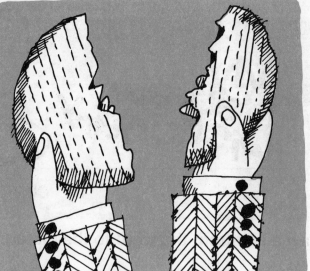

Do you know who I am?
I am the *afikomen,* the piece of *matzah*
    your father hid at the beginning of
    the *seder.*

Did you notice where he hid me?
    Am I under the cushion of the rock-
    ing chair?
    Or behind the oil painting on the
    wall?
    Or between the pages of your big
    book of stories?
If you didn't notice, look for me after the
    seder meal.

When you find me, give me back to your
    father
    so that he can go on with the *seder*
    —and he will give you a special gift.

My Hebrew Dictionary

אֲפִיקוֹמָן

ah-fi-ko-men

AFIKOMEN

Underline the correct answer.

An *afikomen* is a _____.
- *chalah*
- candy
- piece of *matzah*

Father _____ the *afikomen*.
- hides
- paints
- sews

The *afikomen* is hidden during the

_____ .
- ballgame
- concert
- *seder*

When you find the *afikomen* you get a

_____ .
- report card
- present
- pat on the back

Draw a line from the word to the picture.

GRAGGER
SHOFAR

AFIKOMEN
CUP OF ELIJAH

Cross out any letters that appear three times in the box below.

Rearrange the letters to form the name of something which we hide during the Seder.

A	T	C	W	U	E	Y
W	D	V	Z	W	T	S
V	D	O	D	M	S	R
C	Y	S	Y	Z	B	N
K	B	C	T	U	U	Z
F	R	V	B	I	R	•

83

BOW AND ARROW

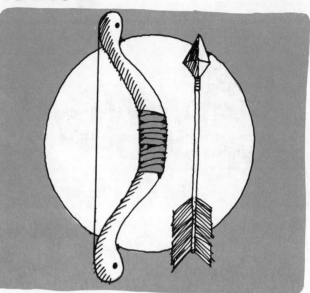

I am a bow and arrow.

When the Romans ruled Palestine, long long ago, there was a sickness among the scholars of the great Rabbi Akiba. The sickness ended on Lag Ba'omer. So you remember that day (the 33rd day of the *omer*) as a day of joy.

You remember Bar Kochba too. He and his brave men fought with bows and arrows to free the Jewish people from the Romans.

Put an arrow in your bow—and let fly!

Shoot me into the sky. Have a picnic, run races, and take hikes.

Today is Lag Ba'omer and your class is out in the country, celebrating the scholars' festival.

84

My Hebrew Dictionary

קֶשֶׁת וָחֵץ

ke-shet
chetz

BOW and ARROWS

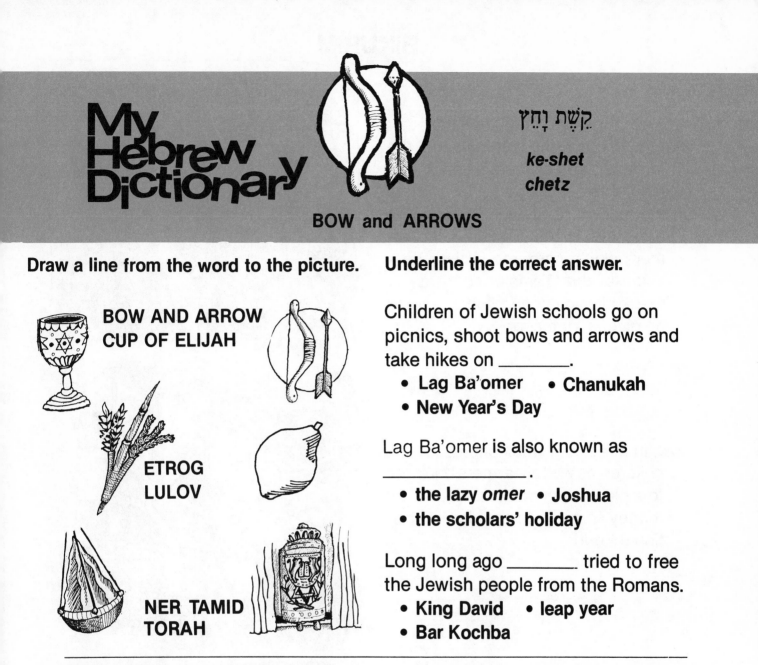

Draw a line from the word to the picture.

BOW AND ARROW
CUP OF ELIJAH

ETROG
LULOV

NER TAMID
TORAH

Underline the correct answer.

Children of Jewish schools go on picnics, shoot bows and arrows and take hikes on _____.
- **Lag Ba'omer**   • **Chanukah**
- **New Year's Day**

Lag Ba'omer is also known as
_____ .
- **the lazy *omer***   • **Joshua**
- **the scholars' holiday**

Long long ago _____ tried to free the Jewish people from the Romans.
- **King David**   • **leap year**
- **Bar Kochba**

Below you will find a box of letters. Find and circle the words in the word list. The words can be found by reading forwards, up and down and on the diagonal.

ELIJAH,

LULAV,

ARROW,

ETROG,

BOW.

T	A	B	L	O	O	L	S
A	R	R	O	W	A	U	E
R	A	T	O	W	M	L	T
A	T	O	R	A	M	A	R
E	L	I	J	A	H	V	O
D	I	M	G	B	I	M	G

85

BIKURIM

I am the *bikurim,* the first fruits that the farmers harvested each year in the land of Israel, long ago.

On the festival of Shavuot they would bring me to the Temple. The farmers would carry me in their baskets to the Temple court as a thanksgiving offering. Later I would be given to the poor.

Now, in Israel, the week after Shavuot, children as well as farmers bring me to a place where I am sold: and the money is given to the Jewish National Fund.

On Shavuot, I am part of the Confirmation ceremony. Carrying flowers or a basket of fruit, each girl and boy walks down the aisle of the temple and leaves me on the *bimah.*

I am also part of another name for Shavuot: *Yom Habikurim,* Day of the First Fruits.

My Hebrew Dictionary

בִּכּוּרִים

bi-ku-rim

BIKURIM

Underline the correct answer.

Bikurim are _____.
- **Two Purims**
- **giant urims**
- **first fruits**

Long ago *bikurim* were brought in a basket to _____.
- **the seashore**
- **the Temple in Jerusalem**
- **the public library**

In Israel *bikurim* are sold and the money is given to _____.
- **the Jewish National Fund**
- **the Tobacco Institute**
- **the Society to Prevent Freckles**

On Shavuot girls and boys carry the *bikurim* to the _____ of the temple.
- ***bimah***
- **water fountain**
- **book shelves**

Draw a line from the word to the picture.

BIKURIM
HAGGADAH

DRAYDL
SUKKAH

Cross out any letters that appear three times in the box below.

Rearrange the letters to form the name of something which we bring to the Temple during the holiday of Shavuot.

B	D	Y	H	W	X	E	D
A	I	A	J	C	W	Y	H
G	F	K	E	F	G	M	F
E	W	C	U	Y	I	A	X
C	J	H	X	R	J	D	G

THE TEN COMMANDMENTS

When God gave us to Moses, He said that whoever would obey the Commandments would live happy lives. The children of Israel promised to obey us.

Today people all over the world try to obey us.

We are the Ten Commandments:

1 I am the Lord your God, who brought you out of the land of Egypt, out of the house of bondage.
2 You shall have no other gods but Me.
3 You shall not swear falsely.
4 Remember the Sabbath day and keep it holy.
5 Honor your father and your mother.
6 You shall not murder.
7 You shall not be unfaithful to your husband or your wife.
8 You shall not steal.
9 You shall not tell lies about anyone.
10 You shall not want what belongs to someone else.

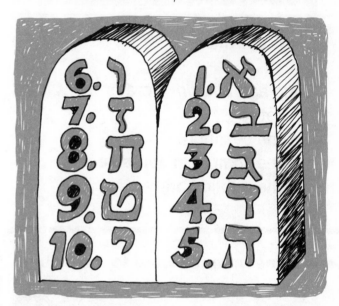

After the children of Israel had left Egypt and were camping in the desert, Moses their leader went up to Mount Sinai. There God give him the Ten Commandments.

My Hebrew Dictionary

עֲשֶׂרֶת הַדִּבְּרוֹת

ah-ser-et ha-dib-rot

TEN COMMANDMENTS

Underline the correct answer.

After the children of Israel left the land of slavery, God gave _____ the Ten Commandments.
- **Moses**
- **Abraham**
- **King Solomon**

Today _____ try to obey the Ten Commandments.
- **only the Jewish people**
- **only the American people**
- **people everywhere in the world**

The Fourth Commandment is _____.
- **You shall not murder**
- **You shall not steal**
- **Remember the Sabbath day and keep it holy**

The Fifth Commandment is _____.
- **Honor your father and mother**
- **You shall not tell lies about anyone**
- **You shall not eat cookies in bed**

Draw a line from the word to the picture.

AFIKOMEN

HAVDALAH

TEN COMMANDMENTS

BIKURIM

On Jewish holidays such as Sukot, Chanukah, Passover, Purim, and Shavuot, we greet our family, friends and neighbors by saying, "*Chag Samayach.*"

"*Chag Samayach*" means "Happy Holiday."

Stand up, shake hands with your friend, and say "*Chag Samayach.*"

89

13. Mitzvah, Tzedakah, Mezuzah.
17. 10 good, 12 excellent, 14 fantastic.

19.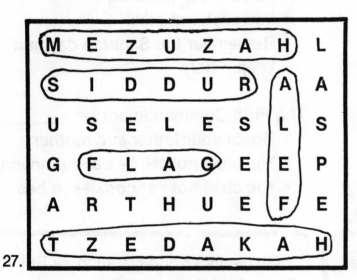

21. 19 good, 21 excellent, 23 fantastic.
23. Tanach

25.

29. 5 good, 7 excellent, 9 fantastic.
33. 7 good, 9 excellent, 11 fantastic.
35. Chalah
37. B

43. Cantor

47. C

49.

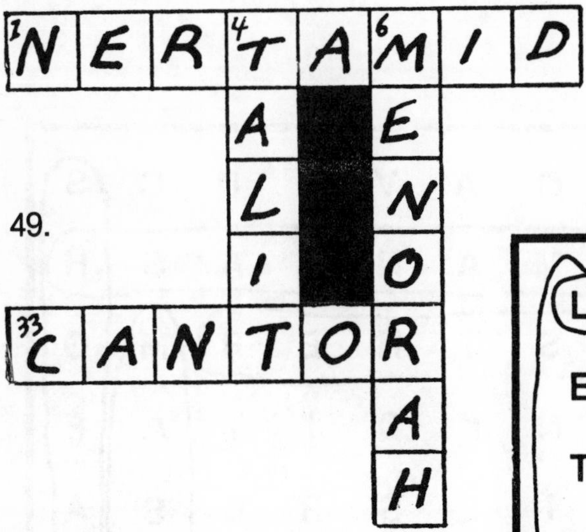

1 NERTAMID
4 TALIT
6 MENORAH
33 CANTOR

55.

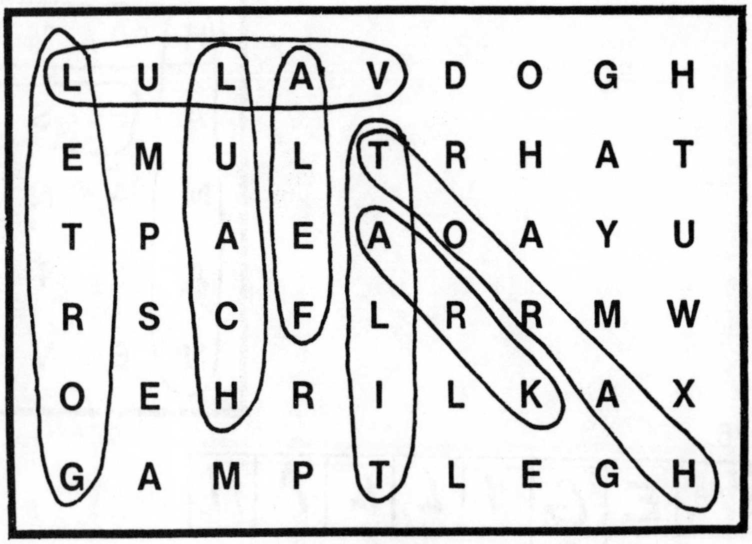

L U L A V D O G H
E M U L T R H A T
T P A E A O A Y U
R S C F L R R M W
O E H R I L K A X
G A M P T L E G H

53. Shofar

57. Sukah, Etrog, Lulav, Alef, Luach.

59. Holy Ark, Havdalah, Mezuzah.

61.

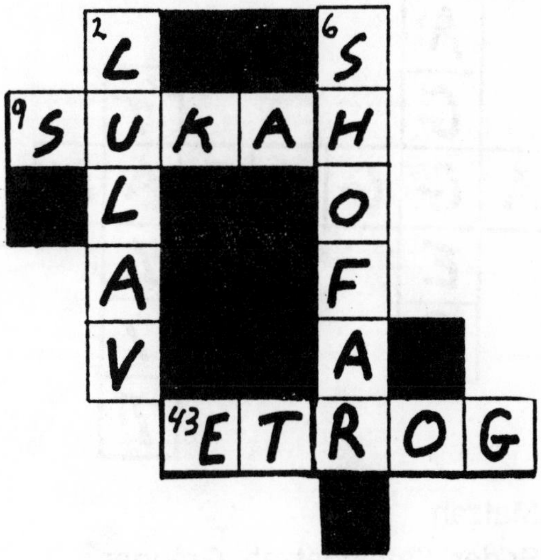

2 LULAV
6 SHOFAR
9 SUKAH
43 ETROG

63. Ten

67.

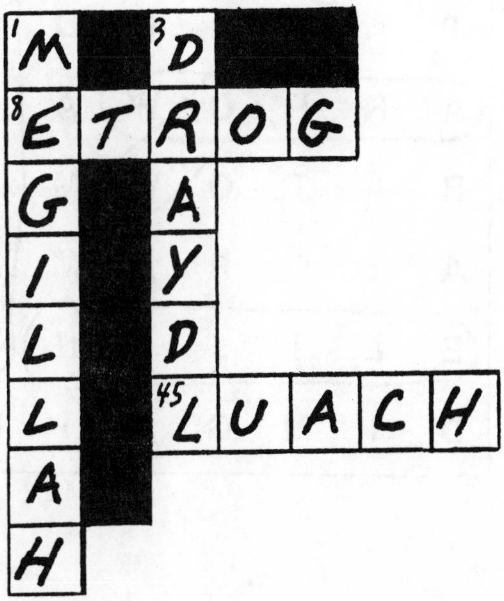

1 MEGILLAH
3 DRAYD
8 ETROG
45 LUACH

69. Gragger, Megillah, Synagogue
71. 11 good, 13 excellent, 15 fantastic

73.

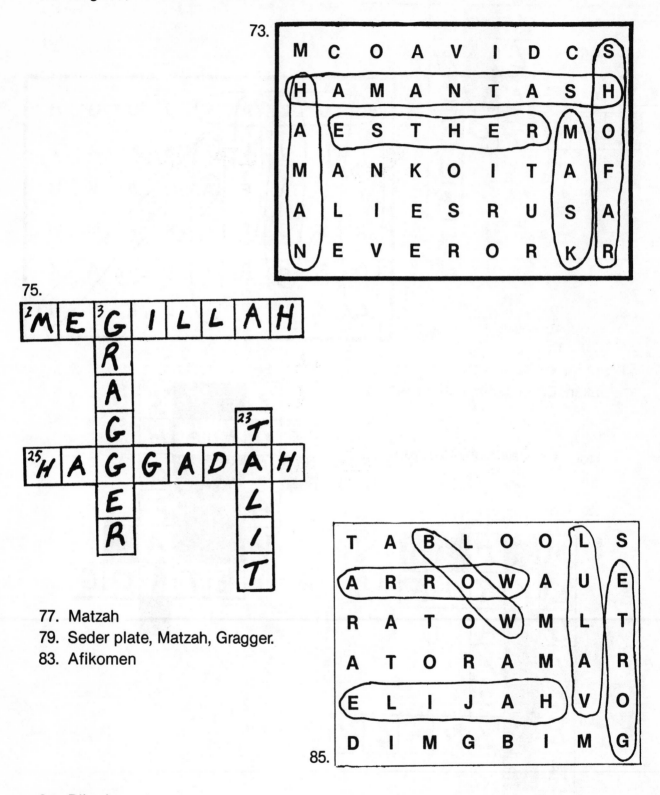

M	C	O	A	V	I	D	C	S
H	A	M	A	N	T	A	S	H
A	E	S	T	H	E	R	M	O
M	A	N	K	O	I	T	A	F
A	L	I	E	S	R	U	S	A
N	N	E	V	E	R	O	R	K	R

75.

```
M E G I L L A H
    R
    A
    G
    G   T
H A G G A D A H
    E       L
    R       I
            T
```

77. Matzah
79. Seder plate, Matzah, Gragger.
83. Afikomen

T	A	B	L	O	O	L	S
A	R	R	O	W	A	U	E
R	A	T	O	W	M	L	T
A	T	O	R	A	M	A	R
E	L	I	J	A	H	V	O
D	I	M	G	B	I	M	G

85.

87. Bikurim